in possession
of loss

Also by M.T.C. Cronin

Zoetrope – we see us moving (1995)
the world beyond the fig (1998)
Everything Holy (1998)
Mischief-Birds (1999)
Bestseller (2001)
Talking to Neruda's Questions (2001)
    [*Respondiendo a las Preguntas de Neruda* (Spanish/English, 2004)]
    [*Controcanto ~ Il Libro Delle Domande di Neruda*
        (Italian/English, 2005)]
My Lover's Back ~ 79 Love Poems (2002)
The Confetti Stone and other poems (2003)
beautiful, unfinished ~ PARABLE/SONG/CANTO/POEM (2003)
<More or Less Than> 1-100 (2004)
The Ridiculous Shape of Longing ~ New & Selected Poems
        (Macedonian/English) (2005)
The Flower, the Thing (2006)
Notebook of Signs (& 3 Other Small Books) (2007)
Our Life is a Box. / Prayers Without a God (2007)
*How Does a Man Who is Dead Reinvent His Body? The Belated Love
        Poems of Thean Morris Caelli* (co-written with Peter Boyle) (2008)
*Irrigations (of the Human Heart) ~
        Fictional Essays on The Poetics of Living, Art & Love* (2009)
*Squeezing Desire Through a Sieve ~
        Micro-essays on Judgement & Justice* (2009)
The World Last Night [metaphors for death] (2012)

M.T.C. Cronin

in possession of loss

Shearsman Books

First published in the United Kingdom in 2014 by
Shearsman Books
50 Westons Hill Drive
Emersons Green
Bristol
BS16 7DF

Shearsman Books Ltd Registered Office
30–31 St. James Place, Mangotsfield, Bristol BS16 9JB
(this address not for correspondence)

www.shearsman.com

ISBN 978-1-84861-382-9

Cover: *Untitled 2003 [Anawhata]*, 2003,
oil on canvas, 1016 x 835, by Antonio Murado.
Reproduced courtesy of the artist and Gow Langsford Gallery.

Australian Government

Australia Council
for the Arts

The author would like to thank
the Literature Board of the Australia Council
for a New Work Grant which was of great assistance
during the writing of this book.

Contents

15   (still alive

16   THE DAWN…
(shall it be

18   THE WORDS…
(your effort seizes you

20   THE STONES…
(what fails

22   THE HOLLOWS…
(how much of what I write

24   THE SCALES…
(hobbled by new cells

26   THE PRAYERS…
(folded, clasped, this belief

28   THE SHOES…
(beneath the war

30   THE SENTENCES…
(no reasons are given

32   THE EGG…
(what remains

34   THE REMAINS…
(I testify that I started out
as a different kind of animal

36   THE SELF…
(when you leave

38   THE SEEDS…
(berries fall out of my eyes

40   THE VISION…
(the baby of the poor woman

42   THE HOURS…
(reasonless

44   THE ROSARIES…
(on a raft of words

46   THE CALL…
(– the mouth

48   THE LAND…
(with what I have written

50   THE MORAL…
(it is the one whose death

52   THE GHOST…
(the breath

54 THE BEGINNING...
    (nerves of spring

56 THE WORD...
    (we have already been dead

58 THE TIME...
    (and so refrain

60 THE SUN...
    (with one small light

62 THE TWINKLE...
    (gentle deception more clear

64 THE SCIENTISTS...
    (there is love that knows infinity

66 THE TOUCH...
    (no beyond

68 THE REMAINDER...
    (who is debt-free

70 THE STORY...
    (we gaze inward at the fence

72 THE MOUNTAIN...
    (between foreign)

74 THE QUESTIONS...
    (in memory of eternity

76   THE END...
        (the only way

78   THE NAMES...
        (only one word

80   THE SAME...
        (our refugees

82   THE LIGHTHOUSE...
        (from the consequences

84   THE MOON...
        (as a lake might be frolicked in

86   THE OCEAN...
        (death proposes

88   THE DARK...
        (I put him into all my arms

90   THE LIGHT...
        (the prayer

92   THE WITNESS...
        (with what the world tells us

94   THE LIES...
        (and so

96   THE SOULS...
        (asleep in your body

98   THE DEAD...
                    (dead

100   THE DREAMS...
                    (time worry

102   THE THING...
                    (the day breath

104   THE HOUSE...
            (when you destroy something

106   THE LAMP...
            (loss is a metaphor for our own lack

108   THE POEM...
                    (epilogues are a lie)

EPILOGUE

113   THE BIRD...

And you, poets, life of this life. You have triumphed over the centuries, despite the cruelty of the eons; and you have won the crown away from the haughty, despite the thorns of arrogance; you have taken possession of the hearts, and your dominion knows no end or cessation, O poets.

KAHLIL GIBRAN

(still alive
we say
but never
still dead)

The Dawn...

Dawn never meant a morning.
Law couldn't say itself enough
to the word stepping out of bounds.
The mathematical equation of the parachute
only sometimes survives landing.
In the cemetery of welcome to the new man
evolution is digging for the gravedigger.
Each clod of earth muffles the sentence:
You cannot say my name without saying your own.
We lose ourselves
between the heart and the mouth.
We lose each other
between the lip and the heart.
Only the word is in possession of loss.
Saving what's lost by naming
all loss as love.

(shall it be
the relations of the dead to the dead
become known
as the eros of forgetting?)

The Words...

then said
then cells blood
then bones teeth
then flesh hair
then time falls out
when all words
are coffins reopened

(your effort seizes you
and carries you to the grave)

The Stones...

sunspoken
sand is tracks' best canvas
sand loses all tracks
today I have written as well
how the stones show me curiosity
because they never open their mouths
save all words by staying
shadeshut

(what fails
your tongue
entreats
and worships
always
without grace)

The Hollows...

We are the hollows.
We are the nest.
We are overfilled.
Excuseless.
In an orchard of fists
we fight each other's motives.
We break our bodies over each other
then cry because it can not be undone.
Fever reminds us of ourselves.
How we are entangled with chaos.
How we are at our own mercy.
Companioned by all proportions.

(how much of what I write
did I think of?
how much of the answer
matters?
these are equal)

The Scales...

A poem weighs nothing.
Innocence bears no record.
The recording hand is heavy.
The wound is inscribed in the heart.
Crawling on all fours through justice.

(hobbled by new cells
your lord continues)

The Prayers...

too many prayers
and too much refusing to pray
too much howling
and too much silence
the game of forever
starts to play out inside your breast
and does not stop
even when you run out of ideas
the rock says
I might be a rock large enough to crush you
and the fire
I might be fire hot enough to burn you
ash is flesh
flesh is ash
simply of another hue
and the ground spits
on what remains of you
while you repeat repeat repeat
your agonizing refusal
and starve yourself
of all other forms of speech

(folded, clasped, this belief
will feed you
you believe, you eat your hands
by mistake)

The Shoes...

On one side of the sun, a gunshot.
On the other, love I made last night.
in limine
In truth, you can't even balance there.
Though we do all our balancing there.
on words
I remove my shoes and put my head in your hands.
Have you ever seen two people turn into one?

(beneath the war
pronouns unfurl
and fall
windless flags
of us)

The Sentences...

The sentences are in love with each other.
All day they fold and throw paper planes.
They eat grapefruit and drink champagne.
They sit in the nasturtiums and shape the underground
into a nest.
They speak about the things that mean a lot to their author
who after much thought or very little
crosses them out.
With the paper they are written on he folds and throws
a miniature plane.
He finds grapefruit bitter and drowns his sorrows.
He sits in the flowers and pretends to be a chicken.
He says nothing to anyone about the egg he lays.
Ah, that he mysteriously lays!

(no reasons are given
for birth
but many for killing)

The Egg...

even an egg
has to put its arms up
sometimes
has to throw them up
in surrender exasperation
frustration
always without words
has to indicate
that an egg
is potential fulfilled

(what remains
in what remains?)

The Remains...

Don't waste time writing something
that's not finished.
Although it seems to be the end
denouement remains.
And the remains are always arriving
according to the memory.
Whatever is born
is already overcome by home.
Where art is a testament
to how beautifully death lives.

(I testify that I started out as a different kind of animal
it took evolution to get me started
it was dreaming of the one creature who couldn't speak his
        own language
and so he mimics
like this)

The Self...

Words catch what falls away from me.
Self abandoning the self.

(when you leave
the air holds the sound
of a black chain)

The Seeds...

all seeds must be abandoned
the little seed in the hard ground
little seed like a hard heart
grab hold of the horns of the moon
white bull of the sky
thread the snails on its glistening saliva
yoke the tree to the pregnant cloud
and speak in an alder voice
rockhole by rockhole
advocate for one hundred years
and another hundred
for those who in spite of love
are forgetful as a thunderstorm
little seed in the heart's hot soil
with plum and worm begin in me
grow the book into a walking man
invite variety to meet the pear

(berries fall out of my eyes
smell of tissues and bones
screams split the sun
into one thousand heads
facets of this tiny fly
watching its own back)

The Vision...

Your vision contains things
which are not in it.
Seeing the baby
you rush to comfort yourself.
The door opens
and there appears to be no door.
Your view extends all the way
to the view and back.
The only end this has
is you can see all of it.
The only true image
is the image of another thing
that thinks itself.

(the baby of the poor woman
has put its fist
through her bladder and bowel)

The Hours...

the hours of our shadow
single-shadow
we exist only in our likeness
all singled out together
for the end

(reasonless
great with the forgotten
actually silence
or silence in its actuality out of relation to sound
it lasts)

The Rosaries...

the rosaries of wine
the willingness in the sun
the old friends grown old
the shadow of a person over a person
the nine lines that began nine times
the apostrophes of winds
the history of cock-a-doodle-dos
the seems to me of the grass
the butterflies of doubt
the beliefs and their fences
the grain, circle, blueness, lung and bait plotting beauty
the little happening voice
asking for its candid mate
the word that gathers together the universes

(on a raft of words
the lips swim
to the island of the heart)

The Call...

on a loss-strange path
in a little city of words
lies a dog-and-man story:
is it home that dreams
of a language that listens
and comes when you call?

(– the mouth
to one's mouth
across the fantastic and imprecise
foreign valley
of time –)

The Land...

the land published as a bestseller
the critics with their greasy tongues forever adjusting the public
the stockmarket subtracting prophets from our dreams
the metaphor lassoed and dragged on its knees through language
the whale made small by the desires of men
the scholar of drudgery never minding his own business
the million forgotten swallows reflected in the mirrors of the void
the prayer knocking down god's door and finding not-god
the lust for the lust for god
the impatient skeleton no longer comfortable even on soft grass
the corpse the cause of all foetal dreams
the remains of the remains counting the profits of the dead
the new commandments found in a wishing well

(with what I have written
everybody gamble)

The Moral…

The moral does not survive the moralist.
What does a knot in the wood secure?
What are you doing with that measurement in your hand?
A plumb holding a plumb.
Never make what will mock you.
If you think something lost would make you less, *lose it*!

(it is the one whose death
you think diminishes us more
who knows that all deaths
diminish us the same)

The Ghost...

The ghost of the tree
haunts the tree.
The ghost of man
haunts men.
Waiting spills from death
and bursts to life
all around us.
Overfilled
we live anywhere
inside the ghost-line.

(the breath
under the song
that delivers the song
beyond death)

The Beginning...

simple as no companion
a walking stone
refusing all crimes
the hell direction
saving inanimately
for the impossible event
the beginning of life
from something
with no idea

(nerves of spring
wonder-working)

The Word...

The word from which the word comes.
That we live in evil.
That the dog need not know god to be mired in faith.
That the spider's early web will wed the dew.
That we saw what was.
That we emit time only from our ideas.
That the star of our nightmares is inhabited only by rats.
That every war is a raw wound.
That seeing merely a part is a trap.
That a ton of not makes no difference to a child.
As a tub of but makes even less.
As yes balances on no.
Meanwhile the moon grows in a ditch and dislodges a rock.
The devil reserves a sin for the next to be born.
The bell of a cramped little bed peels in sleep.
Tears cry for the sad sadness.
The word from which the word comes says itself.
Tomb-talk...
The word from which the word comes writes itself.
Dear read...
Now is always won now.

(we have already been dead
now is not a legacy)

The Time...

this time appropriate
this time not bound by anatomy
this time a door with no wall
this time these are your people
this time the body-less lives
this time a single polysemous meaning
this time the rule not following itself
this time all wrongs lost
this time each in its best spot
this time nothing rewritten
this time only this account
this time a bright shining purpose
you cannot separate what falls
and what does not fall

(and so refrain
and this is my refrain)

The Sun...

the sun that grows this wood in my eye
this sun that buries you
is a child on my lap laughing
is how we took the coffin and put it in the earth
sorrow is how time plays as it ages
is a child on my lap burying the coffin full of laughter
that is this sun wiping the wood from my eye
this sun in the earth
your sun in the earth

(with one small light
in your hand
you think
you can supplement
the night sky)

The Twinkle…

are we not even started?
that twinkle
is it you?
or you?
the little bit that goes up
is it a mountain?
did you mean a song
from how the world
got in your head?
have you not even begun
though you already
have a memory
and another morning
to barely make it
over the collapsed hump
of what your heart
called yesterday?
and there we are
finally all ourselves
how you are when you never
even got going
not never again but never
that twinkle

(gentle deception more clear
than the most surprising thing;
the provocative wonder
of what might and what is possible
riven from what isn't)

The Scientists...

the scientists
have been asking about the soul-triggers
about the doors with no walls
about the crystal ball
in which you will only see
the memory of oblivion
they need a new hypothesis
about the distance between truths
because they thought that love
was inexact

(there is love that knows infinity
because it is felt for the dead)

The Touch...

I will always
be saying this grief.
As death
is continuing.
Estrangement
that comes with words.
Death touching
all life's edges.
Words with which all things
have been named.
In which life agrees
to feel the touch.

(no beyond
the impossible passing
further than the originary to what is bygone?
reach)

The Remainder...

Body,
prophet of loss,
foretells the remainder
with words spoken only by the dead:
Chaos is not this;
meaning is in common.

(who is debt-free
owing everything
to everyone?
it is the same one
whom everyone
borrows from)

The Story...

I won't paint pictures of outlaws and criminals.
I won't paint indigenes' portraits.
I won't write plays about what it's like on the seedy streets.
I won't write a novel based on historical events you claim
          as your own.
If you want the past served up to you as art
go get an 'artist' who'll pander in colour.
If you want to feel like you have a history
find a 'poet' whose craft is to be convincing.
If you want someone else to tell you the story of yourself
find a storyteller who believes who you are.
I'm not going to cram the past into the present.
I'm not going to capitalize on the narratives of identity.
And so I'm broke.
But not broken.
Not like those asses who are so popular
they get ridden all the time.

(we gaze inward at the fence
too high and wide
for the dry black leaps of our heart)

The Mountain...

The mountain fell down
the mountain and landed.
The wind unsearches.
The sea unclaims.
A chance to win
isn't.
The biggest secret
is the one we all keep.
The poet knows not what it is,
poetry.

(between foreign)

The Questions...

are there only old ways of being god?
are we the understanding of down?
plato gazing into a soul to know his soul?
is this the beginning of algebra?
is that the ground falling away?
saviour?
saviour?
saviour?
are those the tolling bells of desire?
is the conclusion just this?
endlessly?

(in memory of eternity
we forget
lest we)

The End...

The end of the day is the end of the night.
The very walls and floors pretend to be walls and floors.
Keening rises from them as if from all fours.
Countries stir and move across continents.
Prayers for war patter like a billion drops of rain.
With the strength of a river they drown out god's objections.
As fear spreads screaming shifts its gender.
Over-bellied women squat and their babies fit where they fall.
A child is need ripped from surviving flesh.
So many cowards to nurture a hero.
Begging the world for a road he is given another man's shoes.
These take him.
One step closer to nowhere.

(the only way
to take charge of living
is to lose hope)

The Names...

Not in our name
this heavy eden
pretended ecstasy
Not in our name
these ruins inside words
barefoot alphabet
indiscreet pastorals
Not in our name
these heart-scars
wrong-way-lookers
impatient faith
this trick prattling
unchoosing
Not in our name
the names of those
who eluded
our denial
Who let only
the complete world
pass their lips

(only one word
could they recognize
but it was the word
whose true meaning
is to be misunderstood)

The Same...

Poker gets played at other tables.
Hiding in murder are the unwitnessed memories.
Bitterness in words becomes more bitter.
Love says nothing so you can say everything.
The same soul works for everyone.
In a stare-off with a rooster sunrise wins.
Tomorrow is surrounded by the sharpest barbed wire.
With(out) a conscience the stick becomes a spear.
There are whole words (woods) that don't care.
Of all the different ways, this is the same as all the others.

(our refugees
no longer visit us)

The Lighthouse...

the lighthouse
inside your
dark house
warns you
of the night
a black hat
for each star
a black hat
for each star
only moon
sky's host
shines earthly
warns you
to unbless me

(from the consequences
of our limited perception
we are protected
by faith)

The Moon...

the moon losing its secrets
to a sea of stars
says where there is a man
someone dies
they die reading the little book
in the hands of an angel
hovering in the light
of the future's promise:
death suffers the worst of the living
new sun new day

(as a lake might be frolicked in
and rinsed with dog
the child crawled back inside me
and pressed her stamp all over me)

The Ocean...

If you've never noticed
that the ocean is composed
entirely of flowers then
I guess it is possible that
you might once have drowned.

(death proposes
not the end of time
but its depth)

The Dark...

A small black spot in the night sky.
A star come loose.
What can only be read in the dark.
God's final draft of loss.

(I put him into all my arms
what had everything on the stars
even numbers
as well what I did
then was decided by the purpose of being
left as each gathers up itself
and all my arms unhold him)

The Light...

God is missing from every breath that forms his name.
God is for those who are gifted with blasphemy.
Shine like gold under the light he wears on his little hat.
The hat likes every head and the well will never lie to the bucket.
The true answer to the prayer is regardless.

(the prayer
is third person)

The Witness...

the witness to the trifle
told them about it
he witnessed a trifle
and he spread the word
which became thin

(with what the world tells us
we evolve into silence)

The Lies...

It's only truth now
looking around
Only ease
kindly articulated
I am not lost
as all the lost have found me
How gratefully
the lies fold up their tongues
Stop telling

(and so
remembering
when it perfects itself
as being)

The Souls...

the warriors' souls
crack like thin sticks over their generals' knees
the tree's soul
is always dressed as a bride
the atheist's soul
is a lynchmob
the souls are signs of waking
and leaving the dream alone

(asleep in your body
is the last bit of time
woken, you are fully alive
as is all that is dying)

The Dead...

the dead
kidnapped by the dance
unfinished dance
neverending

(dead
you can't forget)

The Dreams...

there is a sound made by paradox
there is a dance of the green fruit
a wonderful translation of falling
& every single art thing in the world
there is a title for the living & a sign
that points in the direction of hell
there are little hunters of big prey
& motives stored like the sun
in shining armour and hot blood
there is your body-without-story
parting the furniture from the floor
a dog swallowing a satin ribbon
& a hand-held stick in a new game
there are women's hands sinking
in the chick-gulls' salty down
& an orchard of fish walking
the plank of a farmer's schemes
the limit here is about forever
& you are a silver moth balancing
between death row & a skyscraper
vertical wings joined on the ridge
of a leaf to pray for ceasing prayer
always the subject is shrieking –
most men being proficient in dreams
whether dreams are to be had or not

(time worry
weaves itself into their heads
while they sleep
the trial begins
in their fund of love)

The Thing...

We are already touching
the thing from their country.
We touch it our whole lives
yet it is we who are bruised.
The thing from their country
feels like not wanting to die.

(the day breath
and the night breath
tangle
coroners of the earth
breathe
between what approaches existence
and what exists
no more)

The House...

'All visitors to this house will marvel,
once inside,
that they cannot recall its surrounds.'
When all is forgotten
the nerve sheathes itself
in a place without echoes.

(when you destroy something
you don't understand
you destroy something else)

The Lamp...

The lamp that flickers out is my lamp
I do not want the smoke's answer
I listen to the dead through a stick
I refuse to be *informed*
My dreams no longer dream
I am at my own mercy
How impossible any absence of me
No more arguments
Only longing

(loss is a metaphor for our own lack
unnecessary lack
what you have lost is fixed in loss
what can never leave you)

The Poem...

the poem
completes the poet

(epilogues are a lie)

Epilogue

The Bird...

The streamy babble
of the smallest bird
upon the far-off sound
of midday.
Lucid tree, lucid stone, speaking
through the madness of wind
standing ground.
Where is the eagle
which has killed the cock
in a sky that spins
ever earthward,
where a child's head gentles
a pillow
as night undoes?
Only to-be-forgotten dreams
remember the moon
in the skulls of wary deer
along the fence
or the last task
of the final evening
before this death.
Two leaves, two eyes,
admit dawn
and the sun agrees
to this final reason –
the waking cry of the first bird
is good enough.